GRIT, DISCIPLINE, PERSEVERANCE

The Emotional Habits That Drive Success

Steve Williams

i

are for clarifying purposes only, and are owned by the owners themselves, not affiliated with this document.

CONTENTS

Introduction

If you browse through the interviews with some of the most successful people on earth, you'll find one piece of advice shared by virtually all of them: They never give up on their goals. Research shows that grit is a better predictor for success than any other factor.

The ability to keep going despite setbacks is more important than your IQ, character or other external factors, like your upbringing or surroundings.

But, what does it really mean to "never give up"? What exactly is grit? How do you persevere when face with larger than life difficulties? How do you keep going when you're at the brink of exhaustion, and all your hard work hasn't been rewarded yet?

I wrote this book to explore the subject of persistence from a point of view that is more than just cliché self-help sayings. I want to share with you exactly how to stick to your goals, according to the peak performers and science. Not vague motivational advice that claims we have unlimited strength once we're motivated enough.

By making it the goal of this book, I assume you already have a powerful motivation to work on your goals, yet you find yourself rapidly approaching the point of giving up. Together we'll explore how to push through obstacles and stay tough, even when you've yet to get the taste of the reward you're after.

When you finish this book, you'll possess a whole slew of tips and tricks to keep you going when you want to give up. You'll understand which behaviors will threaten your goals, and which ones will help you stay on course. Last but not least, you'll be able to tackle challenges that would make the average person scream and yell in frustration.

Chapter 1 - What Is Grit, Discipline and Perseverance

In order to understand how to develop grit, discipline and perseverance, you first have to understand what they are. In this chapter, I want to discuss a bit about each of these, and what they mean in your life.

Grit is defined as courage; it is the strength of one's character. Grit is accepting the circumstances that you are in, and accepting them without crying or whining about it. A person that has true grit is a person that accepts their own reality, and never wishes that they were someone else. However, this does not mean that a person does not work hard to change the life they have into the life they want. Grit is the ability to be tough and resilient, always able to pick yourself back up and start over when things do not go the way you planned. It is the ability to not crumble when things get hard.

There was a time when having grit was necessary to survival. If you wanted to go anywhere, you had to walk or ride a horse, you grew your own food, and if you did not, you starved. Sitting down and crying simply was not an option.

Today, however, it seems that those with true grit are a rarity instead of the norm. Vanity is the opposite of grit, and the two simply cannot coexist. Vanity is nothing more than excessive pride.

You see, we live in a time when we are constantly comparing ourselves to everyone else. We compare out houses, we compare our cars, our families and our bodies to everyone else's in the world. Grit cannot exist in a person that is constantly comparing themselves to others, and neither can true happiness.

Think about that one person you know, the one that, no matter what happens in their life, always seems to get back up and keep on going. These are the people that so many of us look up to today, however, this is how all of us should behave. The reason that these people seem to have the strength to keep going all of the time is because they have a purpose in life, they have meaning in their life, and they are constantly growing.

Discipline, or self-discipline is the ability to overcome your own feelings and your own weaknesses. It is the ability to know what has to be done, and do it, even if there are temptations along the way. A person that is self-disciplined does not give in to these temptations, but continues on their path.

A person is not born with self-discipline, but has to develop it over time. The problem is that many people have no idea how to develop it. There is also the idea that self-discipline is very hard to attain, and requires the person trying to attain it to deny themselves.

Another reason for a lack of self-discipline is simply laziness. People would rather be comfortable in their lives, they would rather be cozy and lazy than uncomfortable and working hard to get what they want in life. Self-discipline requires effort, and very few people today are willing to put forth that effort.

There are, of course, many other reasons for the lack of self-discipline, including a fear of failure, inability to pass up temptations, low self-esteem, no purpose in life, procrastination, and poor health.

Those who are self-disciplined, have a set of rules, morals, codes and laws internally that they live by. They do not need someone telling them what they should be doing all of the time, because they already know, and they do it.

According to Time Magazine, those that practice self-discipline are much happier than those that do not. You see, while it is easy to think of a person that is self-disciplined as a person that is uptight and does not know how to have fun, a study that was published in the Journal of Personality showed that, in fact, those who practice self-discipline are most likely to be the life of the party.

The study also showed that those who practiced self-discipline were much happier than those that did not. The reason for this is because a person who practices self-discipline takes care of the important stuff first, and does not put themselves into a situation that would be problematic for them.

Perseverance can be defined as failing 19 times, but still getting up in order to try and succeed that 20th time. It is not giving up when doing something, no matter what challenges are faced or how difficult things become.

It is the ability to reach your goals, no matter how many times you fail. Perseverance is essential if a person wants to be successful in life. When a person has perseverance, they can essentially succeed at any goal they set. However, perseverance does take faith in one's self.

Think about Thomas Edison, he himself said, that he had not failed, he had just found 10,000 ways that did not work. Imagine where we would be today if he had not persevered through the failures, and hadn't continued to work toward his goals. The world would probably be quite a different place than it is right now. You see, a person that has perseverance, knows that they can complete their goals. If a person does not believe in themselves and their ability to complete the goals that they set, they will not have the perseverance to see things through till the end. It is this faith in one's self that gives the person motivation to push onward when they fail at reaching their goals the first time.

Grit and perseverance both can be thought of as the stick-with-it type of attitude, and self-discipline can be thought of as what gets you there. The three work together, and one does not work without the other.

If you only have perseverance, the ability to keep going after you have failed over and over, you are just going to keep failing if you do not have self-discipline. After so much failure, if a person does not have grit, they may begin to feel poorly about their circumstances, and begin to blame other people for the type of life that they are living.

So, how are we supposed to develop grit, discipline and perseverance? In the next chapter, I am going to talk about how to develop grit, discipline and perseverance. Later in the book, we are also going to talk about habits, and how they affect your goals, as well as how you can ensure your success in life.

Chapter 2 - Developing Grit, Discipline and Perseverance

Studies have shown that grit is actually more important than intelligence, skill or talent when it comes to success in life. However, grit is not some special gift that some people are born with while others can never attain. Instead, it is something that we all can learn.

The first thing that you need to do in order to develop grit is to get passionate about what you are doing. Many people think that they cannot develop a passion for tasks that they simply do not enjoy right now, however, it is not about enjoyment, it is about being passionate in everything that you do.

You see, many of us work jobs that we simply do not enjoy. Those that have true grit often work hard in every area of their life, whether it be at home, at work or at school and they are passionate about everything that they do.

In order to develop a passion for the things that you do, you need to take a step back and look at your personal values. These are the things that are most important to you in your life. The next thing that you should look at is one situation in your life, such as your job. Think about the last time you really felt satisfied with what you were doing.

I'm not talking about being proud or boisterous, I'm talking about the last time you came home from work, and knew that you did everything you could do in order to provide for your family. I'm talking about the last time that, no matter whether you enjoyed your job or not, you knew you did your best work possible and worked really hard. Think about how that made you feel.

Now, I want you to think about what your future would be like if you put forth that much effort every single day of your life. Chances are, you would have more job security, you would feel more financially stable and you would know that your family would be provided for. I bet those are feelings that you enjoy.

You see, you don't actually have to love the situation, you just have to love some aspect of it. You have to find something in the situation that you are passionate about and focus on that.

The next step in developing grit is to practice. Any time that we want to accomplish something, we have to practice. For example, if you want to wake up an hour earlier each morning, you're going to have to practice this. There are going to be times that you will be hitting that snooze button, and so sometimes you are going to fail, however, with practice comes success.

Don't stop. In order to develop grit, you have to jump right in. This is not something that you can take baby steps with. So, no matter what happens, you have to resolve to never stop. No matter how hard things get, no matter how much you want to lay down and quit, you have to keep going. It is this idea that does help people develop grit.

Most of the people that you know who display grit, are the ones that have had no choice but to keep going. They are the ones that knew if they gave up, everything would fall apart. You have to develop that same mentality.

Too many people are floating through life right now, no goals, no determination and no purpose whatsoever. When they face adversity, they give up. You do not want to be that type of person!

When people tell me how lucky I am to have the life that I have, I know that I can look them straight in the eye and tell them that luck had nothing to do with it. I had no choice but to become who I am and it was all done through hard work and grit.

Self-discipline is the next topic that I would like to talk about. It is often thought of as something you are either born with or not, and there are tons of books out there on this topic alone.

However, what I have found is that people make the topic seem so complicated that it seems unattainable.

Many people think about the word discipline and instantly feel negatively about it. They think of it as something that is bad and unenjoyable. However, to those that practice self-discipline and truly understand it, it is freedom.

It may seem strange to talk about self-discipline this way, but stick with me and I guarantee, you're going to agree with me. Those that lack self-discipline are slaves to food, sleep, television, money and everything else that is going on around them.

Imagine a person that lacks self-discipline trying to get out of bed in the morning. The alarm goes off, they know they should get up and get ready for work, yet, they also know they can hit the snooze button. This continues on until they are almost late for work, but it really doesn't matter, because they know the worst that is going to happen is that they'll be late for work and won't get paid for that time.

On the other hand, a person that practices self-discipline wakes with the alarm or even before it goes off. Even though it may not be enjoyable, they get out of the bed, shower and start their day, arriving to work on time.

This is just one example a lack of self-discipline can lead to unemployment. Moreover, it can lead to obesity, poverty, depression, and laziness. Before a person knows it, they have become a slave to these problems. However, these problems are not something that a person who practices self-discipline has to worry about.

I have had many conversations where people tell me that they didn't do something, because they didn't *'feel'* like it. This immediately told me the person I was talking to lacked self-discipline, because when you practice self-discipline, you don't focus on what you *'feel'* like doing in any given moment, but instead on what *needs* to be done. You use your brain instead of allowing your emotions or even your body to direct your actions. It doesn't matter if you don't 'feel' like doing something, it doesn't matter if you're tired or just want to relax. What does matter is what *needs* to be done.

Often times, those who practice self-discipline will give up some pleasures in life. They will pass by those thrill-of-the-moment times, because they know that there are other things to focus on.

This, however, does not mean that you have to be boring and never have any fun. It does mean that you will be putting important tasks that need to be done ahead of having fun, and you will only focus on pleasure and fun when everything else is taken care of.

Self-discipline begins with self-knowledge. You have to begin by understanding what your current habits are, because you have to be able to stop yourself from behaving according to the way that you feel, and, instead, ensure that your behavior is based off of what you think.

It is right now that you need to decide which behavior best reflects the goals and values that you have in your life right now. This requires a bit of self-analysis, and it is most effective when you write it all down.

I challenge you right now to sit down with a sheet of paper and write down what your goals, ambitions and dreams are. Write down what you value, and what is important to you in your life.

The next step in developing self-discipline is to develop conscious awareness. If you want to be self-disciplined, you have to consciously be aware of not only what you are doing but of what you are not doing as well. Think about it like this, if you are not aware of the undisciplined behaviors that you exhibit, how are you ever supposed to change them?

As you practice self-discipline, you need to be able to catch yourself when you are displaying undisciplined behaviors. For example, surfing the internet or playing on Facebook when you know that you should be working, biting your nails or even eating that extra helping at dinner time are all behaviors that are undisciplined, and that you need to be able to catch yourself doing.

As time goes by, this awareness of what you are doing will be coming earlier and earlier every time, eventually you will catch yourself before you ever take part in the behavior, which will allow you to redirect yourself and avoid the behavior altogether.

The third step to developing self-discipline is simply committing yourself to self-discipline. It is not enough to simply write down your goals; if making a list of what we wanted to do was the way to get them done, no one would need self-discipline. You have to make a commitment to yourself as well as to your goals in order to accomplish them.

If you do not make this commitment, it becomes very easy to make excuses for not doing what you need to do. For example, if you do not make the commitment to get up at 5 am and workout, it is very easy to hit that snooze button and tell yourself that you will start tomorrow, while snuggling up in bed.

It is also important for you to make this commitment because eventually the initial rush or enthusiasm is going to fade when it comes to any goal that we have set or any task that we have taken on. When this happens if you have not made a commitment to see the project through to the end, you are going to struggle and possibly quit.

If you have a hard time with commitment, simply begin by deciding that you are going to follow through, and do what you say you are going to do. Not only in regard to the time you said that you would do it, but also the way you said you would do it.

After you have done this, I suggest that you begin tracking how often you actually do what you say you are going to do. You are either going to see that you do follow through with what you say you are going to do, and don't really have as much of an issue with commitment as you thought you did, or you are going to realize that you don't do what you say you will.

Either way, when you track this, you are going to find that you begin to improve, doing what you say you will do more often and not committing to tasks that you know you cannot complete.

Next, you need to focus on having courage. Self-discipline can be difficult. It means doing what you know needs to be done no matter how you are feeling. Maybe you are sick, but you know you have to finish a big project, this is where you put your feelings to the side and focus on what is important.

Maybe you are working out and feel as if your arms are turning to jelly. This is where you use self-discipline and keep pushing until you reach your goals.

When you begin practicing self-discipline, you have to understand that there are going to be challenges, there are going to be a lot of forces that are fighting against you. There are going to be days that you are tired, there are going to be times when you are in a bad mood, when you feel as if you are starving or even when you are in pain.

You don't have to pretend that something is very easy for you to do when, in fact, it is not. However, what you do have to do is find the courage deep within you to face these challenges, no matter how difficult or painful they may be.

As you begin to see small victories in your personal life, your self-confidence will grow, and so will your courage, which is going to push you even further when it comes to self-discipline.

Being your own coach is extremely important if you want to develop self-discipline. We all have what is called self-talk, and it can be very harmful or it can be very helpful. The thing that makes the difference is you taking control of your self-talk.

It is your job and no one else's to encourage you and to reassure you. So many people turn to others for this reassurance, and find that they are falling short. People all have their own lives to live, and you cannot expect them to encourage you or reassure you every time you are feeling a bit of self-doubt. It is your job to take matters into your own hands and take responsibility for your own life. You can do this through self-talk.

When you use self-talk, you are able to remind yourself of what your goals are, find courage from deep down that you didn't even know that you had, and it helps you to keep the task at hand in the front of your mind.

When you are struggling and feeling as if you cannot go on, remind yourself that the pain you are going to feel from self-discipline is nothing compared to the pain of regret.

That really is all there is to self-discipline. Even though people try to make it sound complicated and unattainable, it really is that simple.

Finally, I want to cover perseverance and how you can develop it. In order to develop perseverance, you first have to know what you want. This means that you have to create goals.

We will talk about how to create effective goals in the next chapter, but for right now, you need to get specific.

Perhaps you want to lose 20 pounds. That is an okay goal, but it needs to be broken down even more into much smaller goals. How are you going to lose 20 pounds? The steps that are going to get you there need to be the goals that you are going to set, for example, exercising for 30 minutes each morning.

You have to plot out how you are going to reach every single goal and that includes all the smaller goals as well. For example, if you want to lose 20 pounds, one of your goals might be to exercise for 30 minutes each morning, but how are you going to reach that goal? Are you going to wake up earlier? Are you going to cut something else out of your morning routine? These are questions that must be answered if you want to build perseverance, because you have to know what direction you will be going.

You also have to understand that no matter what your goal is, you are going to have to put in time and you are going to have to put in the work. Nothing, and I mean absolutely nothing, in life comes easily, you are going to have to commit to putting in the time and effort that it will take to reach your goals.

The next step is to stop with the self-doubt. I spoke in the previous chapter about how self-discipline required you to have faith in yourself. You cannot have faith in yourself if you are filled with self-doubt.

This means that you have to stop comparing yourself to others. Comparing yourself to those around you is going to lead to self-doubt, because no matter who you are comparing yourself to, you are going to see only the positive aspects of their life while focusing on the negative aspects of your own life.

Instead, you need to focus on *you*. Focus on *your own* strengths, *your own* talents, how far you have come in life and how blessed you are.

You also need to get rid of anything in your life that causes you harm. This can include habits, relationships, or even not taking responsibility for your life. When you are trying to build perseverance, and you have these negative things in your life, you will find that you are always falling back on them. Remove them instead of using them as a crutch and allowing yourself to not reach your goals.

It is important that you also spend time doing the things that you are good at, especially if you have set very difficult goals. The reason for this is because you are going to face failure–that is what perseverance is, after all, picking yourself back up after you have failed, and trying again. When you take part in the things that you are good at, you will be reminding yourself that you do have talents, you do have skills, and you will be building up your self-confidence.

Let it go. It is so easy for us to get caught up and focus all of our attention on the smallest incidents in life. This is especially true if you are a perfectionist. However, it is important for you to learn how to keep your cool when you are under pressure and when the small things go wrong. This is the only way that you will learn how to keep your cool when the big things go wrong, and it is the only way for you to be able to brush yourself off and try again.

When things are going wrong, take a few seconds and step away from the situation. Take a deep breath and count to five before even saying anything. This will allow you to calm down and clear your mind.

It is also helpful if you can write down what is going on, what went wrong and what you think might be a better approach next time. This allows you to see the issue on paper and, often times, you realize that it simply is not as big of a deal as you thought it was.

Finally, you have to just let it go. Time is not going to stop so that you can focus on what went wrong. Life is not going to sit by and wait for you while you pout about your failures. Life is going to keep on going and that is exactly what you have to do as well.

The next step in developing perseverance is to ignore those that are trying to drag you down. It is difficult to understand why some people seem to only want to drag those around them down, but it happens all of the time. One of the reasons that this happens is out of jealousy. You see, when you have dug in your heels and you are ready to make changes in your life, you are going to be met with some resistance from those that are stuck in the same old rut. They can actually become upset with you for taking your life seriously, and those are the type of people that you need to stop.

No matter what goal you set for yourself, there are always going to be those people that tell you there is no way for you to succeed or that you are setting yourself up for failure. This is where a lot of people draw a lot of strength from. They choose to prove wrong those who do not believe that they can succeed at what they have set their mind to.

If there are people that seem to be determined to sabotage your efforts or to ensure that you do not see the success that you are working toward, it is okay for you to eliminate them from your life. You should not be spending time with people like this in the first place.

The next step in developing perseverance is to know what your core values are. Core values are those things that you deeply believe and that are most important to you. These are the values that make us who we are as a person. Family, for example, can be one of your core values, success and accomplishment are a few more. However, there are literally hundreds, if not thousands, to choose from and they are going to vary from one person to the next.

In order to determine what your core values are, you need to spend some time thinking about what is important to you. What are the top three things in your life that you absolutely cannot fail at? Those three areas are a great place to start when it comes to figuring out your core values.

It is important for you to understand what these are, because as you are setting your goals, you are going to have to ensure that they fit in with your core values, and as you choose what steps to take in your life, you want to ensure that they align with your core values.

Finally, if you want to develop perseverance, you have to be able to face reality. This means that when things are not going the way that you want them to go in your life, you need to be able to be honest with yourself and figure out what is going wrong. Are you not doing what you need to be doing in order to live the life that you want to live? It does not matter who you are, if you have ever tried to improve your life and yourself, you have had to face the reality that you may not be doing everything that you should be doing. If you are not able to face reality, if you are unable to be honest with yourself, chances are, you are going to come up with all different types of excuses as to why you do not have the life that you want.

Chapter 3 - Learning How to Set Goals

Goal setting, it is something so few of us actually do, but it is also something that is so misunderstood that, often times, it is not done in a manner that helps us to reach those goals.

Did you know that only 17 percent of the population sets goals? This means that the other 83 percent are wandering around the world aimlessly with no direction in their life.

14 percent of people have some sort of aim in their life, but they have no specific goals written down. This means that only 3 percent of the population actually has written goals that they are working toward.

Studies have shown that those 14 percent that have some type of goal in their mind are more successful than the 83 percent of people that do not have any goals at all, and the 3 percent of people that have written their goals down are more successful than that 14 percent of people who have a goal in mind.

What this means is that by simply learning how to create a goal and writing it down, you will increase your chances of success dramatically.

As you can see from the above statistics, setting goals in your life can be very powerful and it can help to ensure your success both in your personal life as well as in your professional life.

Having goals in your life can be important for many different reasons, but the main reason that people set goals is so that they can become motivated.

When you are setting your goals, you have to ensure that they are achievable. So many people try to set goals, but they create goals that simply cannot be achieved. Of course, this leads to failure and then people give up, never setting goals again. An example of a goal that is not achievable would be losing 30 pounds in one month. However, an achievable goal, would be to lose 8 pounds in a month.

The goal must also be believable. This is simply because if you do not believe you can reach the goal, you are not going to work toward it. For example, if you have never worked out before and you set a goal of exercising for 30 minutes each morning, chances are that you will not believe this goal is even possible. It is not believable that someone who has no experience exercising is going to be able to get up and work out for 30 minutes each morning. However, a much more believable goal would be to work out for 10 minutes each morning.

The factor that you must think about when you are setting your goals is if you are going to be committed to the goal. Setting goals that you are not committed to is simply a waste of time. For example, if you are setting a goal of losing 20 pounds because someone else told you that you should lose weight, however, you are not really committed to the process, you are not going to work toward the goal.

What does it take to create an effective goal? The first thing that you have to consider when you are creating your goals is to ask yourself if it is a measurable goal. You have to set your goals in terms that can be measured, so that you are able to see your progress as time goes by.

Your goals need to be specific if you want to improve, instead of setting what is known as 'do your best' goals or not setting any goal at all. A do your best goal would be, something like this: Do your best to exercise every day.

Now, I can tell myself that I did my best every day, but still was not able to exercise. I can claim that I reached my goal, after all, I did try my best. However, if you want to see results, you have to set specific goals. For example, "I will walk every morning for 30 minutes before I go to work."

This is a specific goal that states exactly what you need to do and how you are going to do it. This goal is also measurable because you will be able to track your progress. You see, your goal may be 30 minutes of walking before work, but you might have to start with 10, adding 5 minutes each week until you are able to walk the entire 30 minutes.

Your goal needs to be difficult but realistic. You need to make sure that your goal is not easy for you to accomplish, but that it takes work. However, you do not want it to take so much work that it ends up being impossible for you to accomplish. A goal should not be so easy that you fail to take it seriously, but it should not be so difficult either that it will cause you to experience a lot of failure. Of course, some struggle and some work is fine, but in the beginning you want to set your goals in a way that will help you build confidence, allowing you to reach your bigger goals.

Setting long term goals as well as short term goals is also very important. Most of the goals that you create are going to be long term goals. It is important for you to break these long term goals down into shorter term goals. For example, your long term goal is to start a business of your own. You will want to create short term goals, such as deciding what type of business you want to start, how to get funding, and so forth.

It is these short term goals that are going to be your road map to reaching your long term goals. Let's look at a long term goal of losing 50 pounds. You will break this down into short term goals, such as, eating 5 fruits and vegetables per day, exercising 15 minutes a day, adding 5 minutes a week until you have worked up to 30 minutes a day, drinking 64 ounces of water a day, and losing 2 pounds per week. By breaking down your long term goals, you have created a road map that will lead you straight to your long term goal.

Express your goals positively instead of negatively. For example, some people will say, "I don't want to be fat," or "I don't want to be broke," or "I don't want to smoke." These are all negative and when you look at these goals written on paper, your brain actually sees, "I want to be fat," "I want to be broke," and "I want to smoke."

Instead, create positive goals, such as, "I will lose 50 pounds," "I will quit smoking," or "I will earn more money." Of course, these are long term goals and would have to be broken down into short term goals, which would also be phrased positively.

Creating positive goals instead of negative ones is going to help you focus on success rather than failure. It will help you to focus on what you can achieve instead of where you have failed in the past.

If you want to determine whether you are creating negative or positive goals, ask yourself if they make you think about what needs to be done instead. A positive goal will give you an idea of the steps you need to take, whereas a negative goal will force you to focus on what you need to change.

Set goals for both your personal and your professional life. Many people find it quite difficult to find balance in their lives. It seems that they are either focusing on their professional life or they are focusing on their personal life, but struggle to focus on both at the same time.

You should never have more than 3 goals for any area of your life and you should have goals for each area of your life at the same time. However, you do not want to set too many goals at the same time, otherwise, you will not succeed at any of them.

Goal Setting Tips

1. Make sure that your goal is your own. While it is great to set goals to improve your life and your health, if you set a goal that you are not excited about, you are not going to have the motivation needed to work towards that goal. It is unlikely that you will achieve a goal that your boss sets for you or one that your spouse sets for you. These are improvements that they would like to see in you, however, when you set a goal, you have to believe that there is some type of pay off just for you, not for someone else.

2. In order to ensure that you have balance in your life, you want to ensure that you are setting your goals in the following areas: Family and home, Finances and Career, Spiritual, Health and

Physical, Social, Mental and Education. Having balance in your life is very important as it will help you to reach your goals. Balance will also ensure that you have a road map in every area of your life, which is very important if you want to get anywhere.

3. Spend time visualizing what it would look like for you to reach your goal. Feel the happiness that you would feel if your goal was reached, imagine how proud of yourself you would be and allow yourself to become motivated by that visualization.

4. Don't just stick to huge goals. Often times, it is the smaller goals that you create that will impact your life the most. Yes, you want to set big goals, but set little ones as well, such as watching 30 minutes less television each day, or taking your vitamins every morning. Sometimes, it is best if we start small when it comes to our goals as well as the changes that we need to make in our life, so that we can build some resolve, preparing us for the challenge of reaching bigger goals in the future.

5. Always write your goals down. I spoke earlier about how only three percent of the population actually writes their goals down. I also spoke about how they are more successful than the rest of the population that either does not write down their goals or does not create goals at all. Not only is it important to your overall success to write down your goals, but it is important to your success in reaching those goals. After you write your goals down, you need to keep them in front of you. Hang them on the wall by your desk or even on your mirror so that you are reminded of them every day. Don't just let them sit in a notebook and become forgotten.

6. Share your goals with the important people in your life. Sharing your goal with those you care about and that care about you is very important to your success. Not only does this make you accountable when it comes to reaching your goals, but it

provides you with a support system. I spoke earlier about people who are going to try and stop you from reaching your goals, and it is important for you to not share your goals with these people. However, this is going to take a bit of trial and error. When you notice that someone is trying to stop you or discourage you from reaching your goals, do not mention your goals to them in the future, but instead find a different circle of people to talk about your goals, so you will get the support you need.

7. In order to ensure that your goals do not become forgotten, it is important for you to check in with your goals regularly and record your progress. There are many goals that you will track daily, such as exercising, however, there are those that you will track weekly, such as weight loss. How often you track your goal is completely up to you, and it depends on the goal that you are setting. You can even keep a journal and jot a few notes down each day about your goals and the progress you made on them. Over time, you are going to find that you are progressing toward your goals and that you are getting closer to completing them every day. When you do not track your progress, it can be very difficult to see the small changes that are taking place, which can become discouraging.

8. Take the steps needed to identify as well as eliminate any obstacles that might get in your way. The fact is, life happens, and there is not a lot that you can do when things get in your way. Emergencies happen, people get sick and for some reason when you set a goal, distractions come at you like never before in your life. Simply writing down your goals and tracking them is not enough to ensure your success. Before you begin working toward your goals, you need to take the time to think about the obstacles that can get in your way. Then, as you are working toward your goals, if you do not think that you are progressing fast enough, you need to take some time and look at what is

stopping you. Always paying attention to the things that are slowing you down or stopping you from reaching your goals is extremely important if you ever want to see success.

9. Avoid making New Year's resolutions. Every year, people ask me what my new year's resolutions are and every year they get the same reply, I have none. This is because I work toward my goals all throughout the year. Creating New Year's resolutions will not only cause you to put your goals off until the beginning of the year but also very few people who create New Year's resolutions actually stick to them. It seems as if it has become a ritual to set these high goals, that we know cannot be reached on the first day of every year, then by the following month, life has gone on as it always has done, and we forget that we even set these goals. Instead, focus on small goals throughout the year, and don't save them all up for the beginning of the year.

10. Create a due date when you are creating your goals. For example, if you want to lose 8 pounds in a month, say, I will lose 8 pounds by such and such date. Setting a deadline is a way to create a sense of urgency, and it will force you to pay attention instead of just letting your goals slid until they are forgotten about.

Chances are, you have a long life ahead of you, and you have two choices when it comes to that life. Either you can begin setting effective goals, finally learning what it is like to be successful, or you can continue to float around in this world with no definite purpose in life hoping for the best. I know what I would choose if I were you.

You see, setting goals is not that difficult and neither is working toward them. It is much less difficult than not knowing what direction your life is going to take or where you want to be in the next six months.

When it comes to goal setting in order for your goals to be effective they have to be created properly, and it is my hope that throughout this chapter you have learned how to do that. Now get out there and start writing some goals!

Chapter 4 - How Habits Affect Your Goals

If you have ever played a sport or taken up a new interest or even set a goal before, you know how great it can feel as you see your performance improving, and you move closer to reaching success or mastery.

What caused you to continue practicing in order to get better and master the new interest? It was good habits; repeating the same actions over and over until you saw the improvement that you desired.

To begin this chapter, I want to talk about how good habits can help you reach your goals. Later in the chapter, we will discuss the ways in which bad habits can stop you from seeing your goals become reality. We are also going to talk about how you can develop specific habits, as well as the different habits that you should develop in order to improve your chances of reaching your goals.

Habits are actions that can be very hard to break at times, because they are so deeply ingrained into who we are as a person. It is an action that we instinctively do without giving any thought to it.

One study has shown that we are not motivated by our goals alone. Yes, it is the creation of these goals that gives us the motivation to begin, but the study showed that it was the habits we have set into place in order for us to reach those goals that gives up the most motivation.

This study found that while a person was working toward their goals, when they took the time to reflect upon the habits they had developed as they were working toward their goals, they experienced more happiness as well as more motivation to continue working toward their goals.

Every habit that we have is triggered by an action or a series of actions and each habit is created because there is some type of payoff. You see, everything that a person does must have some type of payoff, otherwise, they would not complete the task. While it may be a habit for you to scream at your husband when you are feeling upset, you may not see much of a payoff, however, when you really look at the big picture, you are getting some relief from the stress you are feeling and you are able to vent your emotions, and this is your payoff.

Your job is to create positive habits in replace of the bad habits that you currently have. One example, of this might be to exercise instead of screaming at your husband when you are upset. The habits that you are going to be creating, however, need to be in alignment with your goals.

So, if your goal has something to do with losing weight and exercising more, working out instead of screaming would be a great habit to create. The point is that you need to make sure that your habits provide you with a payoff that supports your goals.

If you find that you have habits that are not supporting your goals or that are causing you to stumble when it comes to reaching your goals, you need to replace those habits with habits that support your goals.

You see, it is so much easier to replace a bad habit with a good habit than it is to simply break the bad habit. Think about this, when a person is quitting smoking, they are much more likely to quit if they begin chewing gum or replacing their cigarettes with lollipops. This allows the person to keep their mouth stimulated while not ingesting the nicotine and other poisons from the cigarette. By creating the habit of chewing gum or sucking on a lollipop, the person is replacing their bad habit of smoking.

If you have a bad habit of staying up late and sleeping in instead of getting up early and completing the tasks that you need to get done, you can replace this habit by creating a habit of going to bed earlier and waking up when your alarm goes off. This is especially important if one of your goals is to be more productive during the day.

Think about this. If you could create two, three or even seven habits over the next couple of months, what would they be? Would you break any of the bad habits that you have, replacing them with good ones? Are these habits in alignment with the goals that you have set?

Now, start figuring out how you would create these habits. These are the habits that you need to focus on creating and breaking in your life.

What does all of this have to do with grit, self-discipline and perseverance? Creating good habits is going to help boost your self-confidence, which are going to need when you are developing grit, self-discipline and perseverance. Breaking bad habits and replacing them with good habits is going to help you to develop self-discipline, and because it can be so difficult for anyone to break a bad habit, doing so is going to help you develop grit.

It is important for you to understand that you cannot break or create more than 1 or 2 habits at a time. Trying to do more than this will simply become overwhelming and will cause you to fail. So, how are you supposed to decide which habits you should break or create first? After all, I am sure that you want to create or break plenty of habits.

It is not an easy question for anyone to answer when it comes to what habits you should decide to create or break first. You need to look at what areas of your life need the most change as quickly as possible. For example, if you want to change the way you handle your finances, and you know that if a change is not made quickly, you are going to go under, you would choose the habits that support your finances to work on first. If you know that your health is going to kill you, and you know that changes need to be made quickly, you would choose your health to begin creating and breaking habits.

It is all about priorities, the things that are important in your life, and what needs to be changed in your life.

Now that you know what habits you need to create, you need to learn how to create those habits, and that is what I want to talk about next.

In order to create a habit, you need to first start out by choosing just one habit. As you become more skilled at creating and breaking habits, you can take on more than one habit at a time, but for now let's just worry about the most important habit you need to create. Once you have chosen the habit, you are going to dedicate 30 days to focusing on creating this habit.

While it may become difficult at times, you need to remind yourself that it is really only going to be difficult for the first month, maybe even less. After you make it past the first 30 days, you will have created a habit, and you will be able to move onto the next habit you want to create.

The next step, after committing to the 30-day challenge is to write down what habit you want to create as well as what is motivating you to create this specific habit. You also want to write down what obstacles you think you will encounter as well as the strategies that you will use to overcome the obstacles.

After you create your plan, you will commit to it and begin tracking your progress. In order to track your progress of creating a habit, all you need is a sheet of paper. Write the habit down on the sheet of paper as well as the date for the next 30 days.

On the days that you practice the habit, put a check mark next to the date, and do your best to ensure that every day has a check mark next to it. If you stop practicing the habit for a few days, start over until you are able to go an entire 30 days in a row practicing the habit.

As you work through creating your goal, make sure that you reward yourself each time you make progress. For example, at the 7-day mark, 21-day mark and so on.

Before we move on to breaking bad habits, I want to give you a few good habits that you can focus on creating. These are habits that most people wish they had started with after they have spent years improving themselves and creating new habits.

1. Think positively. This is one of the first habits that you will want to create in your life, because it is going to help you push yourself through the struggles that you will face when creating future habits. Of course thinking positively is not going to ensure your success when it comes to creating other habits. However, by learning to push the negative thoughts out and think more positively, you will learn how to succeed.

2. Start exercising. Of course, I think this should be one of the very first habits that you create, not only because it is good for you and will make you a healthier person but also because it is life changing. When you start exercising, you will find that you have more confidence in yourself, which will lead to more success when you begin making other changes. Exercising also reinforces the habit of thinking positively, because you have to focus on positivity if you want to develop the habit of exercising. Exercising will help to relieve the stress that you are dealing with on a regular basis and will also improve your mental health. When you exercise, you increase your focus and mental clarity. It is during this time that you will find you have your best ideas and are the most creative.

3. Begin single tasking instead of multi-tasking. We have been told so many times that we are supposed to be able to multi-task. There was even a time when those who were able to multi-task were praised for their ability. However, today, we are beginning to understand that those who are actually multi-tasking are not as productive as we once thought they were. Instead, it turns out that since they are unable to give their full attention to one task at a time, they are unable to put 100 percent of their effort into the task, meaning, less than quality work. When you single task, you are able to focus on what you are doing at that exact moment, meaning that you get more done in less time, and the quality of work is improved greatly. Even more importantly, multi-tasking is extremely difficult and very stressful. When you

begin single tasking, you are going to reduce the amount of stress that you have to deal with every day.

4. It is very important for you to create the habit of focusing on one goal at a time. It is so tempting to try and focus on multiple goals at a time, but when you do this, you are dooming yourself to failure. It is understandable that there are a lot of changes that you want to make, however, you need to remember that it is only going to take 30 days to create a habit, therefore no matter what goal you are working on, the habit of working on it will be created in just one month. What this means is that in only a year's time, you will be able to create 12 new habits or reach 12 new goals.

5. Eliminate the things that are not essential in your life. This means that first you must identify what is essential, then begin removing the things that are not needed. This can be things around your home, activities, work projects and even hobbies. Doing this is going to reduce the stress in your life and will ensure that you are able to relax and enjoy life.

6. Become a kind person. Being kind is a habit, it is not something that is naturally within us, and it is something that can be learned over time. Focus on being a kind person every day for a month, make sure that nothing comes out of your mouth that is not kind, focus on having kind thoughts and watch how much your life changes. If you want to develop the habit of being kind, you need to practice it daily and in order to do this, you need to find something kind that you can do for someone every single day. It is best if you do something kind for someone who could never repay you. Also, don't jump onto social media and start bragging about how kind you are, remember, you are not being kind in order to impress or get praise from other people, but you are cultivating a habit and working on improving who you are as a person.

7. Create a daily routine. When you create a routine, it is almost as if you are habit stacking. You will automatically know that after one activity is completed, you are supposed to move on to another specific activity and you will not have to even think about what needs to be done. For example, I know that when my alarm clock goes off, the first thing that I do is make coffee, this automatically triggers me to take a shower, which causes me to dress for the day, fix my hair and brush my teeth. Then, it is time to grab my computer, drink a cup of coffee and start work. Every part of my day depends on that morning routine, my success depends on that routine.

8. Now you do not have to have a routine for the entire day. After I have put in 8 hours of work, I automatically know that I need to do my chores. The rest of my day or the middle of the day is completely free for me to do whatever I want. Routine does not pick back up again until it is time to cook dinner. It is best if you can have a morning and an evening routine, because it will keep you on track and it will help you to reach your goals much faster. The activities that you must complete in order to reach your goals are going to quickly become part of that routine.

Now that you know how important good habits are to your success, it is time for you to learn how bad habits can affect your goals as well.

The truth is, we all have bad habits. No matter who you are or how long you have been working to improve yourself, you are going to have bad habits that you need to break. It does not matter if you have a bad habit of smoking, drinking, procrastinating, biting your nails or overeating, if they are affecting your life, you need to deal with them now.

Whether a bad habit is something minor, such as biting your nails or chewing on your lip when you are nervous, or if it is more damaging, such as putting work off until the last minute or overeating, it can affect how you reach your goals.

The first way that your bad habits affect your success when it comes to reaching your goals is because they send out a bad image. This is not only true for those that are part of your support group, but it causes you to have a bad self-image.

Imagine that you are setting a goal of getting healthy and through accomplishing this goal, you want to inspire those that you love the most to become healthy as well. However, you continue to smoke on a regular basis, even though you are eating healthy foods and exercising regularly. Of course, this is not going to work, because, as you allow yourself to continue to inhale poisons, there is going to be no self-love or self-respect when it comes to your health. This means that when you want that huge piece of chocolate cake, you are probably going to go ahead and eat it, after all, how much more damage could it do than a cigarette? You would also have to consider how smoking would affect you when it comes to exercise. Of course you would not be able to breathe as deeply or as well as a person that does not smoke, therefore you would not be able to exercise as long and you would not benefit from the exercise as much as a person that did not smoke.

This is just one habit out of a list of thousands, but the point is that it can greatly affect the goal. Therefore, before you ever begin working toward your goals, you need to look at the habits you have and determine how they are going to affect your self-image as well as the image your support group is going to have of you.

The next way that bad habits affect your goals is by impacting your progression toward your goal. Take for example the bad habit of procrastination. Now, this is something that everyone has had to deal with at some point or another in their lives, however, if it is not quickly taken control of, it can lead to many problems down the road.

If you are procrastinating at home, it can make you and your family sick, you can lose your relationship and find that friends don't want to come over anymore, because your house is so messy. Procrastination is a huge habit to break and it is important that you do so if you ever want to be successful in life. Procrastination can also lead to depression, which of course is going to push you further from your goals instead of closer to them.

The final way that bad habits can affect you reaching your goals is that many times we don't even know that we have these habits. You see, many times, we become so involved in our own lives, our habits are thought of as who we are, and we really don't take the time to think about how they are affecting us or those that we love. It is very important that you take the time to sit down and think about your habits, how they affect those around you and how they affect you.

Write your bad habits down, write down why you think they are bad, how they are affecting your life and how they are affecting those around you. Then, write down what your life would look like if you broke that habit.

For example, if you have the bad habit of smoking, you might say that it is affecting your life because you cannot breathe well, you are unable to exercise and you are spending too much money. It is affecting others' lives because they have to breathe second hand smoke, you are unable to keep up, and your family does without, so you can buy cigarettes. Finally, you would write down that your life would change if you broke the habit, because you would have more money, you would be able to breathe better, you would be able to exercise more, and you would be able to keep up and play with your children.

Getting rid of the bad habits is very important if you want to be successful at reaching your goals. Of course, you are not always going to catch every bad habit and you are not going to notice many of the smaller habits, however, it is those huge habits, drinking, smoking, procrastinating and so on.

Is there a way to break bad habits that really works? Over the years, many people have worked really hard trying to break their bad habits, however, what most people have found is that they are unable to break the bad habits they have developed over time. But, there is hope. To finish up this chapter, I want to spend some time focusing on the steps that you should take to break the bad habits that you have developed.

The first step in breaking any habit is identifying what your triggers are. Every habit is triggered by something. I spoke previously about habit staking and how after completing one task you will be triggered to move on to the next task immediately, that is essentially what happens with bad habits as well.

What situation triggers the bad habit that you are trying to break? Remember that you will only focus on breaking one bad habit at a time, however, it is important for you to understand what your triggers are for all of your bad habits.

For each trigger that you identify, define exactly what you are going to do instead of taking part in your bad habit. For example, if you know you procrastinate when you become tired, possibly spending time playing games on your phone in order to try and clear your mind, you may choose to get up and go for a walk when you become tired instead of wasting your time playing games.

procrastination, because if procrastination is a habit for you, then you understand how it will only cause you to keep putting off working toward your goals.

Not only that, but procrastination can be detrimental when it comes to other areas of your life, such as your job or even your home. If you have gotten into the habit of putting off projects for your job until the last minute, you will not be able to put forth the effort and provide quality work, because you are going to be focused on rushing through the project just to get it done.

Of course, one may look at this as procrastination as well, however, it is a healthy habit replacing a bad habit. When you go for a walk, your energy levels are going to increase and you will be able to get back to focusing on the job at hand much more quickly than before.

For one month, focus on creating new behaviors for each of your triggers. Maybe you have a bad habit of getting angry with your children when they make a mess in your home and tend to yell when this happens. You may have decided that instead of yelling, you are going to walk away from the situation, and meditate before reacting. For the next 30 days, you are going to have to make yourself do this, focusing on your own behavior and replacing the bad habit with new behaviors or good habits.

After 30 days are up, you are not going to have to focus on it as much, because it will have become a new habit. However, if you find yourself slipping back into your old habits, you will need to make sure that you begin focusing on the new behavior once again.

The fourth step is to identify the situations that trigger the bad habit. For example, if you are trying to stop drinking, you would obviously want to avoid a bar, but you might also find that your favorite restaurant is one of the places that triggers you to drink. After you have identified these situations, you will want to eliminate them from your life as much as possible. If your favorite restaurant is a trigger for you to drink, you might consider finding a new place to eat or ordering out instead of dining in.

Step five is to realize that you are going to have strong urges, they are going to come on fast and they are going to be very strong. What you have to understand is that these urges will pass in a matter of minutes. Many times, they will come in waves and the only thing that you can do is to simply go with the flow, and ride the waves until they calm. You can journal, exercise, go for a walk, practice deep breathing or mediate in order to get through when the urges are too strong.

Finally, you want to stay positive. You will have to deal with negative thoughts, no matter how positive of a person you are. What you have to do is realize that you are having negative thoughts and be able to put a stop to the negative thinking as soon as it begins. You need to understand how important it is for you to replace those negative thoughts with positive ones.

Most importantly, if you do fail, which can happen and often does, take some time to figure out what went wrong and create a plan, so that the next time, you will be able to overcome those obstacles. Start again and never ever give up. Continue pushing on and trying to break those bad habits until you are successful, even if it does take six or seven tries, it will all be worth it in the end.

Chapter 5 - How to Keep Going When Things Get Hard

Part of grit, self-discipline and perseverance is that a person is able to pick themselves up when they have failed or when they are struggling, and that is what I want to talk about in this chapter.

The fact is that no matter who you are, you do not like to fail even though you know it is going to happen. No one enjoys failure, whether it be at home, at work, in a relationship or in any area of your life for that matter.

Failing causes pain, it hurts our self-confidence and while the pain may not be physical, it is still very real. Failure can cause other issues in our lives as well, such as financial issues and feeling as if you wasted your time.

What you must understand if you want to develop grit, discipline and perseverance is that failure is a part of life, and if you have never experienced failure in your life, chances are that you are not pushing yourself hard enough in order to reach your full potential.

When you fail, how are you supposed to pick yourself up and keep going? Failure can cause a person to completely give up, to feel as if they are broken and not good enough or as if they will never be good enough. Or, failure can teach a person a lesson, it can help the person succeed later in life. It all depends on how the person looks at the failure and what they choose to do after they fail.

It is very important that you remember that it is usually through failure that we eventually succeed, however, this is never going to happen if you just give up.

Most of the time when people fail they do their best to try and limit the damage that was caused. For example, how many times have you seen exercise equipment for sale online or in a yard sale? Most of the time, this happens because of failure, after all, who would sell their exercise equipment if they had been successful at making the changes they wanted to make, and used it on a regular basis?

This is what usually happens, a piece or two of equipment is purchased, the person intends to use it daily in order to lose weight, become healthy or just feel better. Then, the equipment is put together, set in a corner and eventually it may begin to gather clothes or just dust. It begins getting in the way, the person hates looking at it every day, because it is a reminder of how they have failed. Then, it gets sold. This is what I mean when I talk about limiting the damage that is done.

This type of reaction is not going to get you anywhere. Instead, you need to look at the situation, look at why you have failed, and figure out what was standing in your way. Create a new plan and start over again.

In order to help you get back up and start over again, you have to remind yourself that other people fail all of the time. It may seem as if other people's lives unfold perfectly, and that they never experience any failure, but you need to remember that people are not willing to speak openly about their failures, after all, that would require them to admit that they had failed. They love to tell you about the new job that they got, but they are not willing to tell you that it was only after being fired from three other companies that they were actually able to find a job that fits them.

However, it is important for you to remember that failure is completely normal, and it is something that most people experience multiple times before being successful. I myself have experienced failure, multiple times, there have been times when the failure was so big that it did get me down for a little bit, however, I knew that it was important for me to learn a lesson from the failure, and for me to try again.

The next step is to remind yourself of the successes that you have experienced in your life. You see, this will help you to remember that failing does not mean that you are a worthless person, nor does it mean that you are weak, and it definitely does not mean that you will never be successful in life.

One great thing that you can do is sit down and create a list of the successes that you have had in your life, this way, when you do face failure, instead of having to remember those successes, you can look back at the list you have created. You see, when you fail, a person can begin to think that they fail at everything they attempt, but this list is going to be there to prove to you that it is not true. It will help you build your confidence.

You also need to remember all of your past failures. We have all faced failure in the past and guess what? We have all lived through it. Of course it is not enjoyable for us to think about the times that we have failed in the past, however, by looking at the mistakes that you have made in the past, you are going to be able to remind yourself how far you have come. You are also going to be able to remind yourself that while failing in the past hurt, you were able to make it past the hurt and move on with your life.

Then, it is time for you to make a decision. Chances are, no matter what has happened, you have a decision to make. There has probably been some type of consequence for your failure, however, even after these consequences, you are going to have to decide what you are going to do next.

Imagine that a person has failed in their finances by using a credit card recklessly. Of course, they are going to have to pay all of the late fees, interest and other fees, but they are also going to have to make a decision. The decision is if they should cut up the credit card and pay it off, or they are going to have to choose to keep the credit card and chance using it as they are paying off their debt that they have already accumulated.

It is important that you do not rush to make any decisions. Instead, you need to take your time and make sure that you have as much information as possible. Take the time to really reflect on your failure, understand what happened, why you failed and how you can ensure that you do not make the same mistakes in the future. You also need to determine if what you are doing really is as important as you think it is.

Next, you will want to talk through your options with someone that you can trust. If you do not feel as if you can trust anyone to help you make your decision, write it out on paper. Write down what happened, write down what mistakes were made and write down what you can do in the future to ensure you do not fail again. Then, write down all of your options. After this is done, walk away. Do something that you enjoy, allowing your mind and body to relax, and don't think about the decision that you have to make until the following day.

After a day passes, come back to your notes, take a quick look at them with a clear mind and then make your decision. Of course, you can choose to do nothing and that is a decision in and of itself, but you need to make sure that you are making an educated decision.

Most importantly, you have to choose to learn from the failure, not dwell on it and move on from it.

Many people think there is some type of magical formula that people use in order to not let things get them down, but the truth is that there is not. They have simply decided that they are not going to break, they are not going to allow the things that happen in life or the failures that they face to keep them down, but instead they have decided that they will learn from the past and move on.

Before I finish up this chapter, I want to give you a few tips that you can use in order to pick yourself back up when life knocks you down.

1. Practice self-compassion. So often, we are able to feel compassion for others, but we are unable to feel compassion for ourselves. This is because we hold ourselves to a higher standard than we do other people. We expect that we are going to be able to do everything perfectly. When you are facing a

tough time in your life, it is important that you do not make it even harder by beating up on yourself.

2. Accept reality for what it is. This can be difficult when you are feeling poorly about yourself or when you are facing struggles in your life, however, you need to ensure that you are not making things out to be worse than they really are, and you also need to ensure that you are not in denial about how bad the situation is. Only when you see the situation for what is really is, will you be able to handle the situation properly.

3. Remind yourself that change is a part of life and that it happens constantly for your entire life. Many people believe that things are going to get easier as they get older, yet, what they find out is that the only thing that is consistent in life is change. Things never stop changing, and the only way that you can make things easier for you is to accept that change is going to happen, and learn how to work with the changes instead of against them. Struggling against the changes that are guaranteed to happen in life is only going to make things more difficult.

4. Understand that you don't have to like everything that happens in life. This is something that so many people in life seem to have forgotten. They tend to think that they should enjoy everything that happens to them and that nothing unpleasant should ever happen to them. This is completely wrong, and it is silly for you to even think that you should never face any adversity in your life. You have to understand and accept that things are going to happen in your life that are not going to be enjoyable, and there are going to be things happening in your life that you won't like. That is life.

5. Learn how to let things go. When you hold on to beliefs or behaviors too tightly, or when you hold on to things that have happened in your life too tightly, you are narrowing your focus onto only that behavior, belief or event. You are also draining

your energy when you spend all of your time worrying about an event that you cannot change.

6. Take the time to take a break. Sometimes, when things are not going right and it feels as if everything in your life is falling apart, the best thing that you can do is walk away from the entire situation and take a break. You want to take a break from thinking about the issue, from talking about the issue and from focusing on the issue. Find something that you enjoy doing and spend the day doing it. You will feel better afterwards, you will find relief from the stress that you have been dealing with and you will be able to clear your mind, which will help you focus on the problem much better when the time comes to focus on it again.

Using these tips to help you handle life when times get hard is a great way for you to move past the things that are causing you to struggle in life and move on to greater things. These are the same tricks that most people who display perseverance, fall back on when they are struggling in their lives, and yes, even *they* struggle at times.

Chapter 6 - How to Fail (and how not to)

Success does not happen by chance, it happens because a person is given a chance and they take full advantage of that chance. It happens because of dedication, perseverance, self-discipline and grit.

Failure also does not happen by chance, but it happens when a person is given a chance and does not take full advantage of it, it happens by choice.

The fact is that if you are reading this book, you have the chance to succeed in life, you have the chance to reach all of your goals, and you have to make the choice either to take advantage of that opportunity or not take advantage of it.

In this chapter I want to discuss the reasons that most people fail, and how you can avoid doing so.

1. Many people fail because they do not define success properly. There are three different opinions about success. The first opinion about success is that it is something that you win. Some people look at success as if it was no more likely and no less likely than winning a flip the coin game. They do not think that success has to do with hard work, but they view it more as if it is a game. The second opinion about success is that it happens randomly, or that there are some people who are destined to be successful and there are others who are destined to fail. If a person believes this way, there is really no point in trying to succeed if you think you are destined to fail. The third opinion about success is that success is earned through hard work and by doing what is right. This is of course the proper definition of success.

2. They are confused about what success looks like. For example, many people do not think they are successful when they are paying their bills, keeping the lights on and putting food on the table, they expect more. However, when you really look at the

big picture, that is success. You see, success does not have to mean that you own a multi-million-dollar company. You define success for yourself, and you should take pleasure even in the small successes that you experience.

3. The third reason is because people compare their success to the success of others. Imagine that there are two friends who both have a goal of losing weight. One of the friends is losing weight at a rapid pace while the other is losing it slowly. Although the second friend is experiencing success (they are losing weight), they compare their weight loss to their friend's and because they are not losing the same amount of weight, they simply give up or lose their motivation. This happens in so many different situations, and it causes people to fail every day.

4. People tend to set themselves up for failure as well. Often times, people will set themselves up for failure by expecting too much of themselves; they try to make too many changes all at once, or they are unaware of their strengths and weaknesses. When a person does not really understand what they are good at as well as what their weaknesses are, they may think they have the ability to do something, only to quickly find out they cannot.

5. Negative thinking is also a huge reason that people fail. The fact is that if you do not believe in yourself, you are never going to be able to put forth the effort that you need to if you want to succeed at anything. Negative thinking only allows you to fail, whereas positive thinking is the only way that you will ever be able to see success in your life.

6. The next reason that most people fail is because they have not set clear goals. I talked about goal setting earlier in this book, explaining how important it is for you to set clear goals as well as knowing exactly how you should create your goals. If your goals are not clear, they will not give you any direction to

follow, and you will ultimately fail.

7. Having an unorganized lifestyle is a great way to ensure that you fail at what you set your mind to. I talked earlier in this book about how important it is to create habits and to habit stack in order to create morning and evening routines. If you want to be successful, you have to organize your life. This also means that you need to organize your home, your workspace, and every other area of your life. Doing so will allow you to focus completely on the task at hand, and will ensure that you do not get distracted by the clutter all around you.

8. One of the main reasons that people fail is that they simply give up. Giving up cannot be an option if you want to be successful. Yes, reaching your goals and changing your life is hard, that is why so few people are actually able to do it, but if you want to be successful, you have to make sure that you do not give up no matter what.

9. People often fail because, they are over stressed. People tend to take on more than they can handle, they think that they can deal with the stress that it will be put on them, not understanding that the body and mind can only handle so much. Not only this, but people most of the time do not know how to handle stress. They just allow it to pile on and pile on, not considering handling it.

10. Finally, people fail because of lack of energy. We live in a world where barely anyone eats right, they do not exercise, they are not hydrated and they are not getting enough sleep. When you do not have the necessary energy to focus on the things that you need to focus on or to do the things that you need to do each day, you are going to fail. You are going to miss deadlines, and you are going to find that what you are accomplishing is not up to the standard that you want it to be.

Failing is very easy, there are so many different factors that can cause a person to fail, however, being successful can be easy as well.

If you want to ensure that you do not fail, there are specific steps that you can take.

In order to ensure that you do not fail, you need to start by learning from your mistakes. It is obvious that you want to be successful in life and that you want to stop giving up before you reach your goals, and the way for you to do this is to take some time and look at everything that has happened in the past.

Think about the mistakes that you made, maybe you could not see them at that time, but now as you look back on them, you will be able to tell what went wrong. This is not to make you feel poorly about the mistakes that you made in the past, but instead it is to make you see where you went wrong, so that you can prepare yourself better for the future.

Stop thinking of yourself as a failure. As long as you tell yourself that you are never going to succeed, you are always going to fail, you are never going to lose the weight, you are never going to get a better job and so on, that is exactly what is going to happen.

The reason for this is because as we practice self-talk, when we tell ourselves that things are going to happen a certain way, our subconscious does not care if we want things to happen that way or not, all it hears is the repeated, "I am a failure" therefore it works very hard to prove you right.

Taking responsibility for your life is very important if you ever want to experience success. You have to stop blaming the way that your life turned out on what has happened to you in the past, how you were raised, that you did not get the right opportunities in life or on anything else besides you.

The fact is, all of us have been through something in life that has caused us some type of trauma, some more than others, however, humans are quite resilient and as long as they leave the past in the past, they can move beyond it. You are responsible for creating your own opportunities, you are the one that has to make all of the choices in your life now.

You have to understand that yes, the things that you have gone through in the past do matter, if you take the time to learn from them, however, you cannot allow them to affect the decisions that you make today, using them as a crutch or an excuse for making poor choices or not following through with the things you want to do in life.

Persistence is key when it comes to ensuring that you do not fail. Think about this, a person wants to lose weight, so they set their goals and follow all of the information in this book, however, they fall off of the wagon here and there, having to start over. Have they failed? The answer is no, because they continue to keep trying, they are persistent. The only time that you really fail is when you stop trying.

When people are criticized or when they are given advice, they often fight against it. Those that fight against it the most are usually the ones that know the criticism is true or that the advice needs to be taken. The reason for this is because we don't want other people to be able to give us advice, we want to feel as if we are infallible, and that those around us look up to us.

However, if you want to ensure that you do not fail, you have to listen to the criticism and advice that is given to you. Listening to what others tell you about improving up on yourself, your work or just your life in general is very important, because it shows that you are humble enough to accept that you do not know everything, and you also understand that others are more likely to see your flaws than you are.

 When a person that fails is given advice, they often become hostile, however, a person that refuses to fail will listen to the advice, but will not react. Instead, this person ponders the advice and considers if it is good advice or if it is bad advice. If it is good advice, the person will create a plan so that they can act on the advice they were given.

I spoke earlier in this book about people who do not want to see you succeed and who will go as far as sabotaging your efforts, and I want to make it clear that there are people out there who will give you bad advice, in hopes that you will listen to them and that you will fail. This is why you need to listen to the advice, but not act on it until you have had time to think about it and decide if it is a good advice or not.

If you want to ensure that you do not fail, you have to ensure that you are not becoming distracted. There are some amazing television shows on today, we have the advantages of smart phones that can provide us with hours of entertainment, there are gaming devices, and of course, there are people to distract us. This is not to mention all of the distractions that we can find online, Facebook, Twitter, YouTube, emails, and the list goes on and on.

When you become distracted, you are taking your focus off of what you know is important and you are allowing it to wander to things that really do not matter, nor do they help you get any closer to reaching your goals.

You have to get rid of these distractions. Of course, it is fine to watch a little television or spend a few minutes on Facebook or do whatever it is that you enjoy doing on the internet, but these need to come after the important things are done. Allowing distractions like these to take your attention off of what is important in life is literally setting yourself up for failure.

The most important part of ensuring that you do not fail is making the choice that you are not going to fail. When you decide that no matter what happens, you are not going to fail, you will do whatever it takes to ensure you are successful.

Chapter 7 - How to Succeed

Of course, the opposite of failure is success so in this chapter I want to make sure that you understand exactly what you need to know to ensure your success.

So many books have been written on the topic of success and how to attain it, yet, people are still looking for information, because what they have been told simply is not true.

If you want to be successful in life, you need to first think about the things that you love to do and do them. This is not to say that you should always be having fun, but if you hate your job, if it is something that you do not enjoy doing at all, you will never feel as if you are successful. This means that you need to take a look at the things that you really enjoy in life and find a job that corresponds with the things you enjoy.

In order for a person to truly be successful, they have to stop being afraid of failure. We spent an entire chapter talking about failure, and another one talking about how to avoid being a failure, however, there comes a point in your life where you are going to fail. You have to not fear failure, but be prepared for it, and understand that it is a learning experience. Failure is not the end of the world, but it is one step closer to the success that you desire.

Be the type of person that takes action. When you are a person that takes action, you are going to find that you are always working toward your goals. You need to ensure that you are not wasting any of your time, but that you are making the most of it and using it to work toward the things that you want in life.

While it is normal for a person to want to spend time relaxing, you need to think about the amount of time that you are spending relaxing. If you find that you are sitting in front of the television for 4 hours a day, you need to start taking more action toward your goals and stop wasting so much of your time.

One great way to do this is to start cutting back on the amount of television you watch by 30 minutes per week. During those 30 minutes, make sure that you are working toward the goals that you have set in your life, and you will find that you become more focused on the goals that you have set.

When you find yourself looking for something to do, you need to remind yourself that you are a person of action, and look at your list of goals, then take the next step necessary to reach them.

It is extremely important for you to avoid conflicts, if possible, if you want to be successful in life. When a person is focused on success, they may find that in order for them to succeed, they need the support of the community. If you are known as a person that is involved in a lot of conflicts, chances are you are not going to get the support that you need.

Even if you do not need the support of the community in order for you to succeed, you still need to avoid conflicts as much as possible, because the only purpose conflicts serve is to cause stress in your life.

Obviously, if you want to be successful in life, you need to reduce the stress in your life. Take some time to look at the different areas of your life that cause you stress. Evaluate if each of these stressors are necessary, and if they are not, eliminate them.

When it comes to managing the stress that is inevitable in life, you have to learn how to handle it. You can do this by journaling, by meditating, by using deep breathing techniques, by exercising or by doing whatever activity helps you to reduce stress.

Stress does not only make it hard for us to focus on the things that we need to focus on in our lives, but it can also affect our health. Stress can actually lead to a heart attack, and if you want to control stress, you need to make sure that you are living a healthy lifestyle.

Your body is made to handle a certain level of stress, that is, if you are giving it the proper fuel, hydrating it and making sure that it is getting the exercise that it needs. If you do not take care of your body, you cannot expect your body to take care of you, so if you want to be successful, you need to focus on your personal health.

Not only is focusing on your health going to benefit you in terms of living a longer and happier life, but it is also going to give you the confidence that you need in order to reach your goals in the future.

giving it the proper fuel, hydrating it and making sure that it is getting the exercise that it needs. If you do not take care of your body, you cannot expect your body to take care of you, so if you want to be successful, you need to focus on your personal health.

Not only is focusing on your health going to benefit you in terms of living a longer and happier life, but it is also going to give you the confidence that you need in order to reach your goals in the future.

Don't be afraid of trying something new. It does not matter how long you have been doing the things that you are doing right now, how long you have worked at the same job or even how long you have lived in the same town. What matters is that you are not afraid of trying new things. So many times, people become stuck in a rut, they live the same ole life every single day, always afraid to take any risks or to try anything new. Those people are missing out on so much in life and they are missing out on opportunities that could change their lives.

Finally, you must be willing to work hard. Those people that go through life, thinking that they are never going to have to work for the things that they want, never obtain the things that they want.

Being successful is very hard work. Often times, it means that you will have long days, you will be exhausted when you go to bed and you won't have a lot of free time to spend on your hobbies or off with your friends. However, in the long run, it is worth it, because while you may miss out on a few parties here and there, while you may work long hours and have to spend time focusing on your goals, the payoff is going to be tremendous, it is going to be the life that you want.

There is no perfect road path to success, if there was, I would be more than happy to share that with you, but the path depends on the person taking it. You see, what has led me to success in life is not going to be the same thing that will lead you to success and what will lead you to success is not going to be the same thing that will lead the next person. However, there are common factors in each path and these are the things that I have talked about in this chapter.

Chapter 8 - How to Build Character

Grit, discipline and perseverance are all developed over time and they all play a big part in your success in life, so does your character. Many people believe that you are born with certain traits that will develop your character, however, I say that you are the only one in charge of your character and you can make it exactly what you want it to be.

I remember when I was a child, sitting at the dinner table with my grandfather and looking at the food that was served as if it was from another planet. I was the definition of a picky eater. However, it was my grandfather's words that have stuck with me throughout my entire life, "Eat it, it builds character."

I remember looking at him as if he were crazy, but then he explained to me that in this life, there are things that we have to do even when we do not want to, but when we do these things, our character is built and we become a much stronger, more determined person.

How is a person's character judged? There are many different ways that we judge a person's character, and they include how they behave when they are angry, if they are kind to others, if they are willing to take the blame for their own mistakes, do they show off and do they persevere no matter what comes their way.

Of course, there are many other ways for you to judge a person's character, but just looking at the list above, do you think you are a person of good character?

If you think that your personal character needs to be improved, I have great news for you. By following the steps that I am going to give to you, your character can be exactly what you want it to be.

The first way for you to gain character is for you to get experience in life. As you grow older, your character develops and becomes stronger because you have had so many experiences in life. In order to get these experiences, take risks, get out there and approach that guy that you have been flirting with or go rock climbing or even try new foods. Whatever you do, you have to stop coming up with reasons for you to not try something, start coming up with reasons to try something new.

Become friends with people who are older than you. Spend time with people that do have a lot of experience in life, and take note of the traits you want to develop. Spending time with those that have had a lot of experience in life is a great way for you to understand how character develops as you get older, and it is also a great way for you to see how things can go wrong.

While you are taking note of the traits you want to develop, you might also want to consider taking note of the traits that you do not want to develop as well.

Make sure that you are getting out of your comfort zone at least once per week. When we do not get out of our comfort zone on a regular basis, we end up developing huge fears and we get stuck in our comfort zone. However, when we get out of our comfort zone, we actually expand it, and we quickly learn that we are able to get out of our comfort zone and nothing bad happens.

At least once in your life, work at a job that you do not enjoy and that is not fun. Find a temporary summer job, cleaning hotel rooms or mopping the gas station bathrooms. These jobs will show you what you are made of, they will show you what it is to have perseverance, and you will begin to develop more empathy for those that do jobs like these on a regular basis.

This will also help you later on as you are working toward your goals, because you can use it as a motivator, reminding yourself that you do not want to work that type of job for the rest of your life, and pushing yourself toward success.

Commit to improving yourself. It is so easy to make a list of the things that you want to improve about yourself and about your life, and there is so much information available that you could literally work on self-improvement your entire life and still not read it all. What this means is that no matter what you want to improve in your life, you can find the information needed, and there is really nothing stopping you from constantly working to improve yourself and your life.

Vent in private. One huge character flaw that so many people have is that they vent in public. I'm sure you have seen them, usually in the grocery store or department store, loudly complaining about their day, their life, their spouse or something else in their life. It can go as far as full on arguments. You have to understand that while this may not be uncomfortable for you, venting all of your dirty laundry out in public is very uncomfortable for those that are in the store, and it can be quite a shock to those that witness it.

Don't get angry or throw a fit when you lose. You are not going to be able to be perfect all of the time, you are not going to be able to win at everything you do and nobody likes a sore loser. Instead, congratulate the person that won, tell them they did a great job and move on with your life. Losing is not the end of the world.

You should also remember to not gloat or make others feel bad when you win. Being a humble winner is very important, and it is a character trait that any people need to focus on developing.

Developing your character really is not that hard, and it often happens naturally as long as you do not lock yourself up in your house and never experience anything in life. However, if you want to develop your character faster, simply identify the characteristic that you want to develop and start displaying it.

Developing your character is going to work just like developing a habit does. When you start practicing it, the characteristic will become part of who you are, and eventually you won't even have to think about your actions, they will become natural.

Chapter 9 - Changing The Way You Think

Your success in life is completely dependent on the way that you think. I have mentioned this multiple times before in this book, but I feel it is important for me to finish this book up by talking about how you can change the way that you think.

We have all done it before, we have found ourselves thinking negatively about a situation in our lives, about something that we have done or about failures that we have experienced in the past.

Of course, most of us know one of those people that always seem to look on the bright side and see a silver lining in every cloud. If you are a negative thinker, this will usually get on your nerves and can irritate you very much, but if you find that this is happening, it is a sure sign that you need to change the way you think.

In a perfect world, our thoughts would always be positive, they would always be encouraging us and they would never get us down. But, we don't live in a perfect world, and that is why we have to take control of our thoughts.

That is the first step when it comes to changing the way that you think. You need to understand that your mind is not uncontrollable and that it does not randomly come up with negative thoughts. This happens because you have developed the habit of thinking negatively over time.

In order to take control of your thoughts you have to become aware of them. You have to become aware of the negative thoughts, so that you are able to squash them and replace them with positive thoughts.

For example, you have to become aware of thinking that you are a failure and replace that thought with one that tells you that you are capable of doing anything you set your mind to.

Changing the way that you think is a great way to change the way that you feel about yourself. You are actually going to be able to become more confident in who you are if you focus on changing the way that you think.

You can also take part in guided meditations. These are great to use when you have a bit of down time each day or when you are sleeping at night. These guided meditations are full of affirmations that will change the way your subconscious mind thinks.

Of course, this might sound like a bunch of bull, and that was what I thought of the first time I heard about it, but I gave it a try. At that time, I was working in a factory, the job was very difficult and it was labor intensive. There were many times when I would hear that little voice in my head telling me that I could not go on, I could not keep doing the job.

One day as I was lifting on some products, unloading an entire skid, the same voice started in my head, but this time I had been practicing guided meditation for over a month. So, when the thought of not being able to do the job crossed my mind, a louder voice spoke up immediately and told me that there was nothing I could not do. Suddenly, I was able to unload the skid with no problem. That was the first time that I noticed a difference, and that was 5 years ago. To this day, I still use guided meditations.

You can find these online, many of them are on YouTube, simply search out positive affirmation mediations and you will get a huge list. Give a few a try and find your favorite, listen to it every night when you go to bed or at least once per day as you take part in your normal daily activities, and you are going to see a huge change in the way you think. The meditation is actually working while you are asleep to rewire your brain and change the way that you think.

Changing the way that you think does take some effort, but if you have been living a life full of negative thoughts, taking the time to change the way that you think is going to pay off big time.

Related Reading

I have the perfect complement to this resume building book to further help you succeed in landing the job you want. Getting the interview simply isn't enough. You need to know exactly what to do and say during the process to guarantee you the job.

I highly recommend that you check out my book, *The Successful Interview – 7 Secrets to Landing Your Dream Job*. It is available on Amazon in digital and paper format.

Scan the above code or go here to view on Amazon:
http://www.amazon.com/dp/B011BCYED4/

Stop... Before you close this book, get your free bonus...

Scan Above to Claim Bonus

Or Go To: http://bit.ly/1NKyFuQ

101 Life Success Tips – Start Accomplishing Your Goals Today!

Steve Williams is a motivational expert who has helped thousands of people accomplish their dreams and goals. Here are a few tips he has learned along the way to improving success in his life quickly.

----

1. **Use Visualization.** Visualize what your life will be like when you accomplish your goals. If you cannot see yourself accomplishing your goals, then chances are, you will not accomplish them. Remember that you are to keep your eye on the prize at the

end of the road. There will be times when you feel as if you are stuck and that you are not making any progress toward your goal, but what you need to do when this happens is to remember what your life will be like in 6 months or a year if you continue to work toward your goals. Spend a few minutes with your eyes closed, visualizing how great you will feel and all of the changes that will take place in your life once you reach these goals.

2. **Read Books, a Lot of Books**. For each of these tips, there is a book out there that will give you deeper insight into each tip. Spend time reading each and every day. This will not only exercise your brain and help you learn, but it will also help to relieve the stress you have to deal with on a daily basis. Even if you are not reading a book about self-improvement, make sure you take some time each day to read. Reading fiction books helps to release the creativity we have within ourselves, which can help you solve problems down the road.

3. **Accept That You are Responsible for Your Life.** You are in charge of your life, no one else. You cannot blame your failures on your parents or on what happened to you when you were in high school. You need to work through any issues you may have but while doing so, understand that no one makes your life what it is except you. If you are not succeeding in life, no one has caused this except for you and when you are successful, you will have no one to thank for it but yourself.

4. **Learn How to Accept Failure and *Learn* from It**. Failure, it is something that all of us will face at one point in our lives, no matter what we do to avoid it. You have two choices when it comes to failure. You can either allow the failure to upset you and stop you in your tracks, or you can learn from the failure and change what you do in the future. One example of this may be that you are trying to lose weight, you are tempted by a chocolate cake, and end up eating all of it. Now you have failed. You can either choose to give up on your weight loss goals and eat lots of chocolate cake in the following days, which will most likely cause you to gain more weight, or you can learn from your mistake, understand that you lack the will power to stop eating

after a small piece of chocolate cake, avoid it in the future, and move on with your diet and weight loss plan.

5. **Do the Things You Dread the Most First.** No matter what it is that you want to do, you should always do the things that you dread the most first. This is called eating the frog. This way you are not putting these tasks off while finishing up more enjoyable tasks, you simply do them, get them out of the way, and then you can move on to the tasks you will enjoy more.

This is a brand new report that will show you 101 quick ways to improve your life success. These are just a sample. You can have the entire report for free.

Check Out My Other Books

Below, you'll find some of my other popular books on Amazon and Kindle. Simply scan the link below to visit my author page on Amazon to see my works.

Direct Link - http://www.amazon.com/Steve-Williams/e/B0125EAWUQ/

The Successful Interview – 7 Secrets You Didn't Know About Landing Your Dream Job

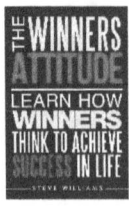

The Winners Attitude – Learn How Winners Think to Achieve Success in Life

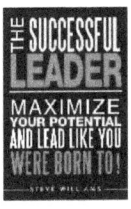

<u>The Successful Leader – Maximize Your Potential and Lead Like You Were Born to!</u>

<u>The Successful Coach – Become the Coach Who Creates Champions</u>

If the links do not work, for whatever reason, you can simply search for these titles on the Amazon website to find them.